Bees and Wasps

Sally Cowan

Contents

What Are Bees and Wasps? 2

The Life Cycle of Bees and Wasps 6

Where Bees and Wasps Live 8

What Bees and Wasps Eat 12

Inside a Honeybee Hive 14

Different Kinds of Bees and Wasps 18

Bees and Wasps in the Environment . . . 22

Glossary 23

Index 24

What Are Bees and Wasps?

Bees and wasps are flying insects that have four wings.

There are thousands of different kinds of bees and wasps throughout the world. Most of them can sting.

European wasp

honeybee

Some bees and wasps have brown or black bodies with yellow stripes.
Others have brightly coloured markings.

Like all insects, bees and wasps have six legs and three main body parts: the head, the thorax and the abdomen. The females usually have a stinger at the end of the abdomen.

These insects have a narrow waist, which allows them to bend their bodies quickly to sting their enemies.

This wasp is bending at its waist to sting someone.

Bees and wasps have **antennae** (say: *an-ten-ee*) for smelling food. They have a tongue for drinking, and sharp jaws for biting, digging and grabbing.

Differences Between Bees and Wasps

Honeybees	Wasps
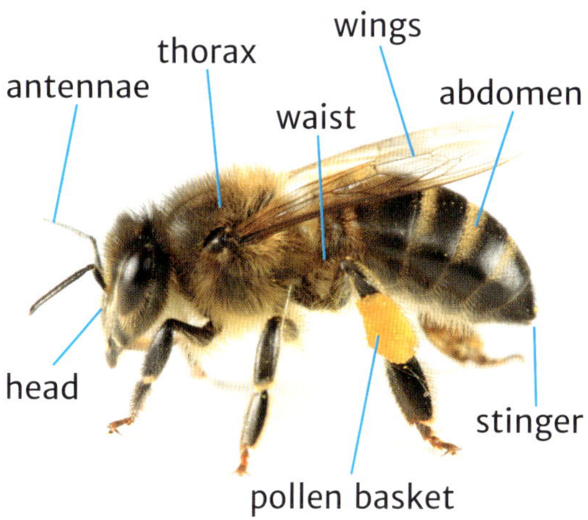	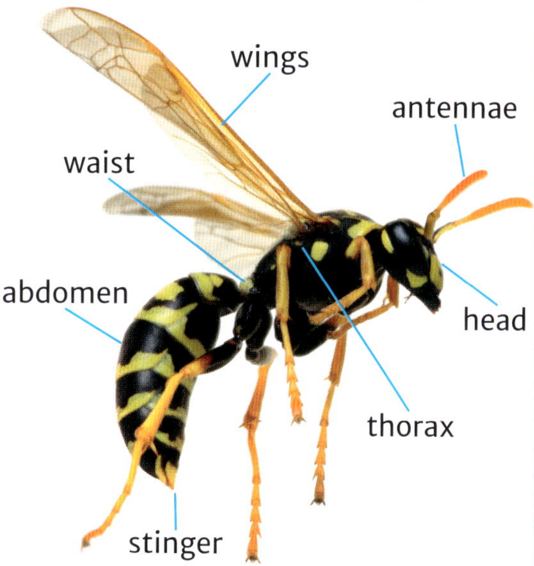
short, sturdy, hairy body	long, thin, smooth body
short, hairy legs	thin, hairless legs
thick back legs with pollen baskets for carrying pollen	long, thin back legs
short, bent antennae	long antennae
Female bees can only sting once.	Most female wasps can sting many times.

The Life Cycle of Bees and Wasps

Bees and wasps have the same life cycle.
There are four **stages** in the cycle.

A female bee or wasp lays eggs in a nest.
Tiny grubs called larvae (say: *lar-vee*) hatch from the eggs.
They begin to eat and grow bigger.

When a larva has eaten enough food,
it forms a hard case around its body
called a pupa (say: *pyoo-pa*).
Inside the pupa, the larva's body changes.

A fully formed adult insect breaks out of the pupa.

This is a bee larva.

The Life Cycle of a Paper Wasp

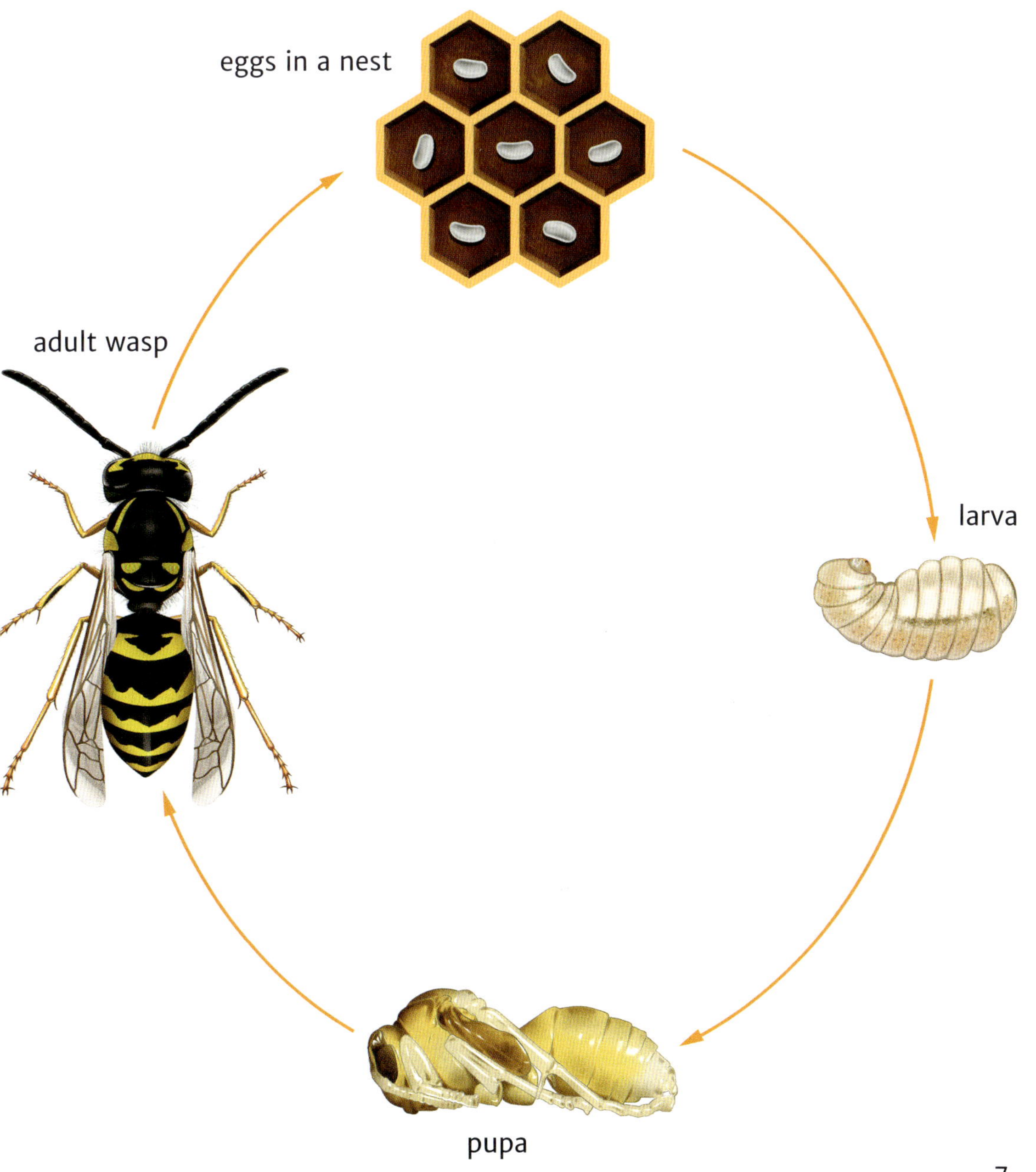

Where Bees and Wasps Live

Bees and wasps live almost everywhere, except in very cold places. Their **habitats** are forests, wildflower fields, farmlands, cities and deserts.

Most kinds of bees and wasps live alone. The bees dig holes in the soil or look for little holes in logs to make their nests.

a carpenter bee inside a hole in a log

a ruby-tailed wasp on a wildflower

Some wasps build tiny nests out of mud,
or burrow into the branches of plants.

Others don't make nests at all.
They lay their eggs in the nests of other wasps.

The potter wasp builds a nest out of mud.

There are some kinds of bees
that live together in groups called **colonies**.
The bees in a colony share their nest, or **hive**.
Thousands of honeybees can live in one hive.
They build the walls of their hives from wax
that **flakes off** their bodies.

These honeybees are building honeycomb.

The walls of the honeybees' nest are formed
from groups of **cells**. Each cell is made of wax
and has six sides. The groups of cells
are called honeycombs. Honeybees use the cells
to store honey and keep their larvae safe.

Some kinds of wasps live together in colonies, too. Paper wasps chew up wood, then spit it out. The wood becomes very soft, like paper, and is used to build the colony's nest.

Paper wasps often make their nests in buildings.

What Bees and Wasps Eat

Bees and wasps cannot eat solid food. They drink **nectar** from plants, but they feed solid foods to their larvae.

Bees gather **pollen** from flowers and carry it back to their nests in pollen baskets on their legs. They store the pollen in the nest for their larvae to eat.

This honeybee is flying back to its nest with a full pollen basket.

Wasps are fierce hunters.
Different kinds of wasps use their stingers to catch spiders, cockroaches, caterpillars and even honeybees for their larvae to eat.

A wasp can sting many times, but honeybees can only sting once before they die.

This wasp has caught another insect.

Inside a Honeybee Hive

A honeybee hive is a busy place!
There are three different-sized bees in a colony: a queen bee, worker bees and drones.
They have different jobs to do.

The queen bee is the largest bee.
Her job is to lay lots of eggs so that there are always enough bees to work in the hive.

Worker bees build honeycomb in a hive.

Most of the honeybees in the hive are smaller worker bees. They gather pollen and nectar from flowers. They feed it to the larvae inside the hive. Worker bees also turn nectar into honey.

Worker bees protect the hive from danger. They sting people or animals that disturb the hive.

The drones are larger than worker bees, but they do not do any work. They eat lots of food made by the worker bees. Then, they leave the hive to **mate** with another queen so that a new colony can begin.

People keep bees to sell the honey that the bees make.

Parts of a Honeybee Hive

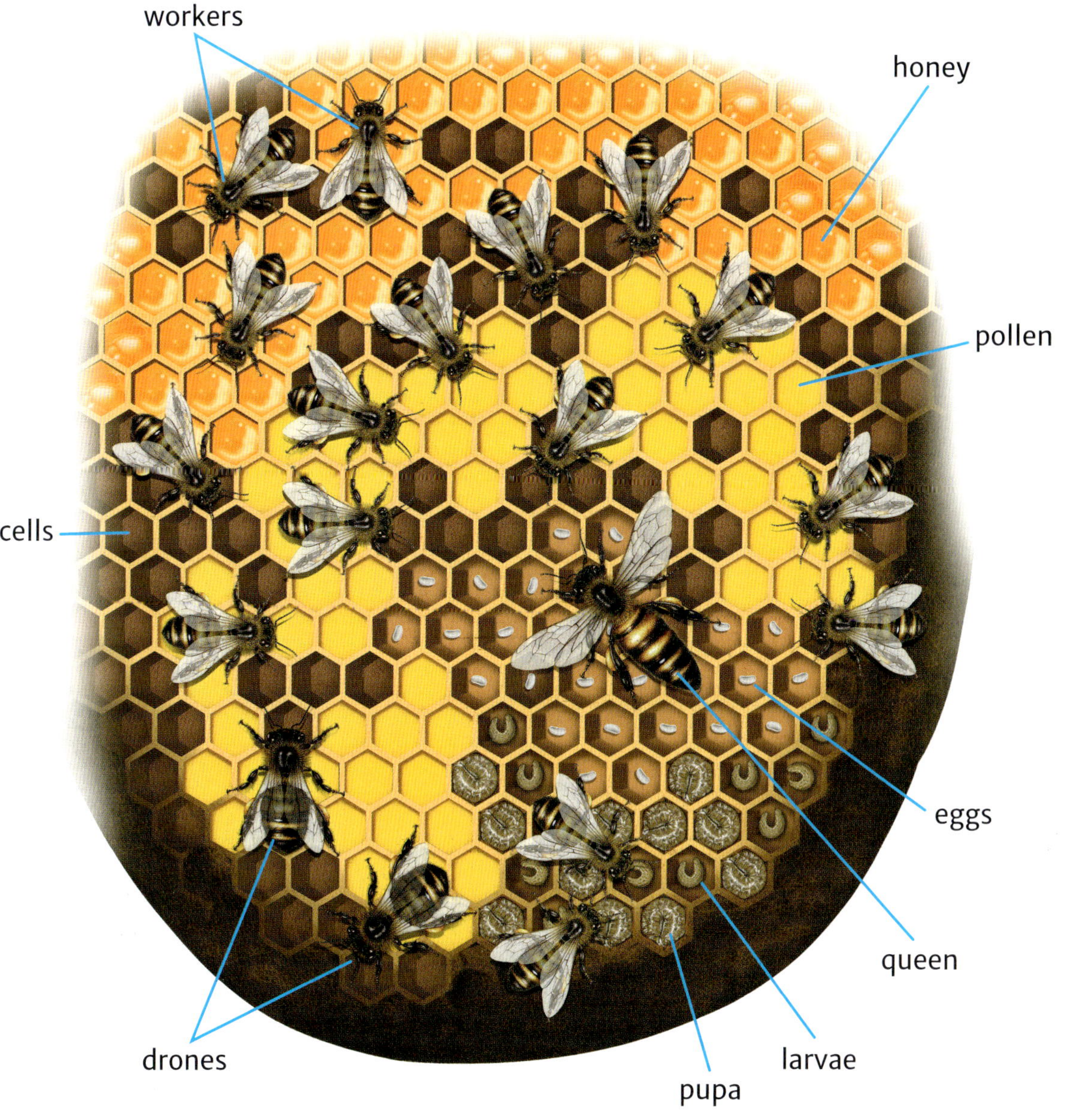

Different parts of a honeybee hive are used to hold eggs, pollen and honey.

Different Kinds of Bees and Wasps

There are many different kinds of bees and wasps in the world.

Blue-banded bees live in most parts of Australia. These bees have a special way of gathering the pollen that is deep inside some kinds of flowers. They grip the flower and shake their wing muscles. This makes the pollen shoot out of the flower.

a blue-banded bee

Leafcutter bees live in several parts of the world. They cut neat holes in leaves with their strong jaws. Then, they use the pieces of leaf to build their nests.

A leafcutter bee cuts holes in the leaves of a plant.

Large tarantula hawk wasps are often found
in the deserts of North America.
They hunt large spiders called **tarantulas**.
After stinging a tarantula,
the wasp drags it back to its nest.
The spider becomes food for the wasp's larvae.

Asian giant hornets are also large wasps.
They live together in colonies
in the warm forests of Asia.
These hornets hunt honeybees and large insects
to feed to their larvae.
The hornet's stinger is 6 millimetres long.

The Asian giant hornet can be 5 centimetres long.

Some honeybees have learnt how to fight off Asian giant hornets.
They work as a team to cover the hornet and kill it.

Bees and Wasps in the Environment

Bees are the best insects in the world
at spreading pollen.
Plants need pollen to grow fruit, nuts and vegetables.

Wasps spread pollen, too.
And if there were no wasps, the environment
would be overrun with other insects and spiders.

It is important to protect the habitats
of bees and wasps, to keep the environment healthy.

Glossary

antennae (*noun*)	feelers or stalks on an insect's head
cells (*noun*)	many small box-like areas
colonies (*noun*)	large groups of the same kind of insects that live together
flakes off (*verb*)	comes off in thin pieces
habitats (*noun*)	places where animals usually live
hive (*noun*)	the nest of honeybees
mate (*verb*)	to make eggs together
nectar (*noun*)	a sweet liquid made by flowers
pollen (*noun*)	the powder that is found inside flowers, which helps to make new seeds
stages (*noun*)	the separate parts of a process
tarantulas (*noun*)	large, hairy spiders

Index

abdomen 4, 5

antennae 4, 5, 23

Asian giant hornets 21

blue-banded bees 18

cells 10, 17, 23

drones 14, 16, 17

eggs 6, 7, 9, 14, 17, 23

environment 22

flowers 8, 12, 23

food 4, 6, 12, 16, 20

habitats 8, 22, 23

hives 10, 14–17

honey 10, 15, 16, 17

honeybees 2, 5, 10, 12, 13, 14–17, 21

honeycomb 10, 15

larvae 6, 10, 12, 13, 15, 17, 20, 21

leafcutter bees 19

life cycle 6, 7

nectar 12, 15, 23

nests 6, 8, 9, 10, 11, 12, 19, 20

paper wasps 7, 11

pollen 5, 12, 15, 17, 18, 22, 23

pupa 6, 7, 17

queen 14, 16, 17

sting 2, 4, 5, 13, 15, 20, 21

tarantula hawk wasps 20

thorax 4, 5

wax 10

worker bees 14, 15, 16, 17